D1245715

A Beginners Guide to

ChatGPT
ENTREPRENEUR'S

Guide to everything you need to Make Millionaire Money with Ai and Prompt Engineering

CHAT GPT GIRL & CHALIE KNOWES

Copyright © 2023 by ChatGPT Girl Notice of Rights

All rights reserved. No part of this book may be reproduced, stored in a retrieval system, or transmitted in any form or by any means, electronic, mechanical, photocopying, recording, scanning, or otherwise, except as permitted under Section 107 or 108 of the 1976 United States Copyright Act, without the prior written permission of the publisher.

This book is protected under the copyright laws of the United States of America. Any reproduction or unauthorized use of the material or artwork contained herein is prohibited without the express written consent of the publisher.

Disclaimer

This book is intended for informational and educational purposes only. The information presented in this book is not a substitute for professional financial or legal advice. The author and publisher make no representations or warranties of any kind, express or implied, about the completeness, accuracy, reliability, suitability or availability with respect to the book or the information, products, services or related graphics contained in the book for any purpose. Therefore, any reliance on such information is strictly at your own risk.

The author may include affiliate links in this book. If you purchase a product or service through one of these links, the author may receive a commission.
The presence of affiliate links does not affect the content or recommendations made in this book.
The author only includes affiliate links for products or services that they believe will add value to the reader.
Please consult with a professional financial advisor or attorney before making any financial decisions. The author and publisher are not responsible for errors, inaccuracies or omissions. They shall not
be liable for any loss or damage of any kind, including but not limited to any direct, indirect, incidental, consequential, special or exemplary damages arising from or in connection with the use of the book or the information contained within it."

Table of Content

Grab Your Freebie!

Bonus 150 Plus: Powerful prompts

You have the opportunity to turn ChatGPT into a money-making, secretary note-taking, personal chef, blog-creating machine, and so much more. The reason we wrote this book is to give you the opportunity to join the rise of AI and allow it to make your life better, one prompt at a time. This book was created with the help of Chatgpt.com.

If you have any issues, email us at info@chatgptpromptbook.com

Grab your Freebie at https://chatgptpromptbook.com/freebie '

Scan the Qr Code to get your Freebie

Introduction

Embracing the AI Revolution with ChatGPT

As the world moves increasingly rapidly, artificial intelligence (AI) has emerged as a powerful force shaping our lives, personally and professionally. From virtual assistants like Siri and Alexa to advanced recommendation algorithms on platforms like Netflix and Amazon. AI has become an indispensable part of our daily routines. The impact of AI is only set to grow as it continues to evolve, offering new solutions to age-old problems and transforming the way we interact with technology.

In the midst of this AI revolution, ChatGPT stands out as a remarkable innovation. Developed by OpenAI, ChatGPT is a cutting-edge language model designed to generate human-like text based on a given prompt. The potential applications for ChatGPT are virtually endless, ranging from content creation and brainstorming to research and communication. For freelancers, entrepreneurs, and professionals of all stripes, mastering the power of ChatGPT can be a game-changer, unlocking new levels of productivity and efficiency.

This book is your friendly guide to harnessing the full potential of ChatGPT in your freelance or entrepreneurial journey. We understand that the world of AI can be intimidating, especially for those who are just starting to explore it. That's why we've crafted this book with a conversational tone, making it feel like you're part of a warm, engaging discussion. Our goal is to make you feel comfortable and included in the conversation, so you can learn about ChatGPT without feeling overwhelmed.

Throughout the chapters, we'll take you on an exciting journey with an overview of ChatGPT's capabilities and a step-by-step guide to getting started. We'll then dive deeper into advanced techniques, tips, and tricks to help you maximize the tool's potential and enhance your productivity. Along the way, we'll share real-life examples, success stories, and practical exercises to ensure you can confidently and effectively use ChatGPT in your daily work.

So, are you ready to join the AI revolution and transform your freelance or entrepreneurial life with ChatGPT? Let's dive in and explore the possibilities together. We'll embark on a journey that will leave you feeling empowered, informed, and excited about the future of AI. We can't wait to share this incredible tool with you, and we're confident that by the end of this book, you'll be eager to tell your friends and colleagues about the amazing world of ChatGPT.

Welcome aboard!

Chapter 1

ChatGPT and You: A Match Made in AI Heaven

Outline
- Personal and professional uses of ChatGPT
- How ChatGPT can improve your work-life balance
- Real-life examples of successful ChatGPT applications

A Warm Welcome to Your ChatGPT Adventure

Welcome to your ChatGPT adventure! In this chapter, we'll explore why AI matters in the entrepreneurial and startup world and how you can harness the power of ChatGPT for both professional and personal use. We'll discuss how ChatGPT can improve your work-life balance and provide real-life examples of successful applications. We'll also share tips on using this amazing tool for various tasks, from social interactions to helping clients and creating other income streams. By the end of this chapter, we're confident that you'll be eager to explore ChatGPT's potential and share your newfound knowledge with friends and colleagues. Let's dive in and discover the incredible world of ChatGPT together!

Why AI Matters in the Entrepreneurial and Startup World

The ever-evolving world of AI has become a crucial component of the entrepreneurial landscape. Offering cutting-edge solutions that enable startups and freelancers to work more efficiently, innovate more effectively, and stay ahead of the competition. With the power of AI at your fingertips, you can streamline your workflow, automate repetitive tasks, and dedicate more time to focusing on your core business activities.

Using ChatGPT for Professional and Personal Use

ChatGPT is a versatile tool with a wide array of applications. Let's dive into some of the ways you can use ChatGPT in both your professional and personal life:

1. **Content Creation:** Generate engaging blog posts, social media content, or

marketing materials with the help of ChatGPT.

2. **Brainstorming:** Use ChatGPT to generate ideas for new products, services, or business strategies.

3. **Customer Support:** Provide timely and helpful responses to customer queries by integrating ChatGPT into your support system.

4. **Communication:** Draft well-crafted emails, messages, or reports with ChatGPT's assistance.

5. **Personal Growth:** Seek advice on personal development, time management, or goal-setting from ChatGPT.

6. **Journaling prompts:** Use ChatGPT to generate daily journaling prompts to help you reflect and grow.

7. **Personalized affirmations:** Use ChatGPT to create personalized affirmations that align with your goals and values.

8. **Self-reflection questions:** Use ChatGPT to generate thought-provoking questions for self-reflection and personal development.

9. **Creative writing prompts:** Use ChatGPT to generate creative writing prompts for personal projects or just for fun.

10. **Meditation scripts:** Use ChatGPT to create guided meditation scripts tailored to your personal needs and preferences.

Improving Work-Life Balance with ChatGPT

ChatGPT can help you achieve a better work-life balance by automating time-consuming tasks and offering valuable insights. With ChatGPT at your side, you can:

- Reduce stress by delegating repetitive tasks to the AI, freeing up time for relaxation and self-care.
- Enhance productivity by focusing on high-priority tasks while ChatGPT handles the rest.
- Improve decision-making by leveraging ChatGPT's insights and recommendations.

Real-Life Examples of Successful ChatGPT Applications

To help you envision the possibilities, here are some real-life examples of individuals using ChatGPT to their advantage:

- A freelance writer uses ChatGPT to generate article ideas and outlines, significantly reducing the time spent on research and brainstorming.
- A startup founder employs ChatGPT to automate customer support, allowing the team to focus on product development and growth.
- A busy professional uses ChatGPT to draft and edit emails, saving time and ensuring clear, effective communication.
- A health coach utilizes ChatGPT to generate personalized meal plans and workout routines for clients, adding value to their services.

Chapter 2

Getting Started: Our Quick and Easy ChatGPT Setup

Outline
- Setting up an OpenAI API account
- A step-by-step guide to using ChatGPT for the first time
- Exploring essential parameters and settings

Welcome to the next exciting step of your ChatGPT journey! In this chapter, we'll guide you through the straightforward process of setting up an OpenAI API account and using ChatGPT for the first time. We'll explore essential parameters and settings to ensure you're fully equipped to make the most of this powerful AI tool.

Let's dive in and set up your ChatGPT account together. These instructions are easy to follow, making it possible for anyone to understand, even a 5-year-old.

Setting Up an OpenAI API Account

1. Visit the OpenAI website at https://www.openai.com/.
2. Click on the "Sign Up" button in the page's top-right corner.
3. Fill out the registration form with your name, email address, and the desired password, then click "Sign Up."
4. Check your email inbox for a confirmation email from OpenAI. Click the link provided in the email to verify your account.
5. Log in to your new OpenAI account and navigate to the API section.

You're now ready to use the OpenAI API and access ChatGPT! Here is a Step-by-Step Guide to Using ChatGPT for the First Time;

1. After logging in, locate the "API Keys" tab and click "Create API Key." Copy your API key, as you'll need it to authenticate your requests.
2. Install the "openai" Python package by running the following command in your

terminal or command prompt: pip install openai

3. Create a new Python file and import the "openai" package: import openai

4. Add the following lines to authenticate your API key: openai.api_key = "your_api_key_here"

5. To make your first ChatGPT request, add the following code to your Python file:

Python Copy code

"text-davinci-002"   "What are some benefits of using ChatGPT?"

50   1   None   0.7
print   .0

6. Replace "your_api_key_here" with your actual API key and run the Python file. You should see a generated response from ChatGPT!

Exploring Essential Parameters and Settings.

Here's a brief overview of some key parameters you'll encounter when using ChatGPT:

* engine: Specifies the model version you're using (e.g., "text-davinci-002").

* prompt: The input text that ChatGPT will use to generate a response.

* max_tokens: The maximum number of tokens (words or word pieces) in the generated response.

* n: The number of responses you want to generate.

* stop: A string or list of strings that, if encountered, will cause the response to stop.

* temperature: Controls the randomness of the generated text (lower values make the output more focused and deterministic, while higher values encourage more creativity).

Paid Option: OpenAI Pricing Plans

OpenAI offers several pricing plans, including a free tier and paid options with additional benefits:

- **Free Trial:** Limited access to the OpenAI API and ChatGPT, suitable for testing purposes.
- **Pay-as-you-go:** Provides more extensive access to the API and ChatGPT, with the flexibility to pay for only the resources you use.

Upgrading to a paid plan can benefit you by offering faster response times, higher usage limits, and priority access to new features and improvements.

In this chapter, we've made setting up your ChatGPT account as simple and enjoyable as possible. By diving deeper into ChatGPT's features and incorporating the AI tool into your daily routine, you can unlock its full potential and enjoy its numerous benefits. Remember, the key to mastering ChatGPT lies in practice and experimentation.

Don't be afraid to explore different settings and approaches to find the perfect balance that meets your needs. Don't forget to grab your free prompt guide. It will help you along this journey that you are embarking on.

Chapter 3

Pro: Tips on How to Get the Most out of ChatGPT

Outline
- The art of crafting effective prompts
- Fine-tuning temperature and other parameters
- Strategies for obtaining desired results

The Art of Crafting Effective Prompts

By mastering the art of crafting effective prompts and understanding how to fine-tune ChatGPT, you'll be well on your way to making the most of this powerful AI tool.

Remember, practice and experimentation are key to success!

Let's Get started! In this chapter, we will explore the art of crafting effective prompts, fine-tuning temperature and other parameters, and developing strategies to achieve desired results with ChatGPT.

1. **Setting clear goals:** It's essential to set clear goals when using ChatGPT. Knowing what you want to achieve helps you craft better prompts, resulting in more accurate and useful output.

Example of prompts and responses:
Prompt: "List five ways to increase productivity while working from home."
Response: "1) Set up a dedicated workspace; 2) Establish a consistent daily routine; 3) Schedule regular breaks and exercise; 4) Use productivity tools and techniques like time blocking or the Pomodoro Technique; 5) Set boundaries and communicate expectations with family or roommates."

Prompt: "What are the advantages and disadvantages of using an electric car?"
Response: "Advantages: 1. Zero emissions; 2. Lower operating costs; 3. Quiet and smooth operation; 4. Potential for renewable energy sources; 5. Reduced

dependence on fossil fuels. Disadvantages: 1. Limited driving range; 2. Longer refueling times; 3. Upfront cost; 4. Limited charging infrastructure; 5. Battery degradation over time."

Prompt: "Suggest five healthy meal options for a vegetarian diet."
Response: "1. Quinoa and black bean salad with fresh vegetables; 2. Chickpea and spinach curry served with brown rice; 3. Grilled portobello mushrooms with roasted vegetables and whole-grain couscous; 4. Lentil and vegetable soup with whole-grain bread; 5. Stuffed bell peppers with rice, beans, and avocado."

Prompt: "How can I improve my time management skills?"
Response: "1. Prioritize tasks using methods such as the Eisenhower Matrix; 2. Break tasks into smaller, manageable chunks; 3. Set deadlines and stick to them; 4. Limit distractions and focus on one task at a time; 5. Regularly review and adjust your schedule based on your progress and changing priorities."

2. **Breaking down complex questions:** If you have a complex question, break it down into smaller prompts. This will help ChatGPT understand your query and provide more accurate responses.

Example: Instead of asking, "What are the steps to start a business?" break it down into:
Prompt: "What are the initial steps to start a business?"
Response: "1. Research your target market and competition; 2. Identify your unique value proposition; 3. Develop a business plan; 4. Choose a business structure; 5. Secure funding."

Prompt: "What legal requirements should I consider when starting a business?"
Response: "1. Register your business with the appropriate government agency; 2. Obtain necessary permits and licenses; 3. Comply with tax regulations, including obtaining an Employer Identification Number (EIN); 4. Understand and follow labor laws; 5. Protect your intellectual property with trademarks, copyrights, or patents as needed."

Prompt: "How can I create a business plan?"

Response: "1. Executive summary: Provide an overview of your business; 2. Company description: Detail your business's purpose, goals, and structure; 3. Market analysis: Research your target market and competition; 4. Organization and management: Describe your company's management structure; 5. Marketing and sales strategies: Outline your approach to attracting and retaining customers; 6. Product line or services

---

Don't forget to grab your free prompt guide. It will help you along this journey that you are embarking on. Don't do ChatGPT alone! Click the link to get yours
https://chatgptpromptbook.com/freebie.

Chapter4

"Making Money While You Sleep: ChatGPT and Passive Income Opportunities"

Outline
- Building chatbot-based products and services
- Monetizing AI-generated content on various platforms
- Affiliate marketing using AI-generated content

In this chapter, we'll explore how ChatGPT can help you create passive income streams by building chatbot-based products and services, monetizing AI-generated content on various platforms, and creating productivity solutions. We'll also discuss affiliate marketing using AI-generated content.

1. Professional Cold Outreach:

Prompt: "Write a cold outreach email to a potential client, introducing your services as a freelance graphic designer."

Response: "Subject: Boost Your Brand with Stunning Visuals Dear [Client's Name],

I hope this message finds you well. My name is [Your Name], and I'm a freelance graphic designer with over (years of experience) in the industry. I came across your company, [Company Name], and I couldn't help but notice the incredible work you're doing in (industry).

I believe that eye-catching visuals are essential for any business to thrive, and I'm confident that my skills in (specific design area) can help elevate your brand to new heights. I've worked with clients from various industries, and I specialize in creating (type of design work) that look great and effectively communicate your brand's message.

I'd love to offer you a (discount/offer) on my services to kickstart our collaboration. You can check out my portfolio at (portfolio website) to see some of my previous work. If you're interested, please feel free to reach out to me at (email or phone) so we can discuss how we can work together to achieve your business goals.

Looking forward to hearing from you soon.

Best regards, [Your Name]

(Your contact information)."

NOTES

Prompt: "As a reader, create your own cold outreach email for your specific profession or service.

Use the following template as a guide:

'Dear (CLIENT'S NAME   ),

My name is (YOUR NAME   ), and I

am a (YOUR PROFESSION   ) with (YEARS OF

EXPERIENCE   ). I came across (CLIENT'S COMPANY

OR PROJECT   ) and (SHARE A GENUINE

COMPLIMENT OR OBSERVATION   )."

NOTES

NOTES

NOTES

2. Estate:

Prompt: "Write an email introducing yourself as a real estate agent to potential homebuyers, focusing on your expertise and commitment to finding the perfect home."

Response: "Subject: Finding Your Dream Home with [Your Name] Hello [Potential Homebuyer's Name],

My name is [Your Name], and I am a licensed real estate agent with (years of experience) in the [Location] market. I am passionate about helping people like you find their dream homes and am dedicated to providing exceptional service throughout the home-buying process.

I specialize in (type of properties) in the [Location] area, and my local knowledge and expertise will be invaluable as we navigate the market together. Whether you are a first-time homebuyer or looking to upgrade, I am confident that I can find a property that suits your needs, budget, and lifestyle.

To begin our journey towards your dream home, please feel free to reach out to me at (email or phone) so we can set up a time to discuss your preferences, requirements, and any questions you may have about the home-buying process.

I look forward to working with you and helping you find the perfect place to call home.

Warm regards, [Your Name]

(Your contact information)."

Prompt: "As a reader, create your own introductory email for your specific profession or service in the real estate industry. Use the following template as a guide: 'Hello (RECIPIENT'S NAME   ), My name is (YOUR NAME   ), and I am a (YOUR PROFESSION   ) with (YEARS OF EXPERIENCE   ) in the (LOCATION   ) market. I specialize in (TYPE OF PROPERTIES OR SERVICES   ) and (SHARE YOUR UNIQUE SELLING PROPOSITION   ).'"

NOTES

3. Passive Income Section: Creating an eBook with ChatGPT

To create an eBook that generates sales, you can use ChatGPT to help you brainstorm ideas, outline the content, and even write the book's actual content. Here's a step-by-step guide:

Brainstorm eBook ideas:

Prompt: "Generate a list of 10 eBook ideas related to (YOUR NICHE   )." Choose a topic and create a working title:

Outline the eBook:

Prompt: "Create a catchy title for an eBook about (CHOSEN TOPIC   )."

Prompt: "Create an outline for an eBook about (CHOSEN TOPIC AND TITLE   )."

Write the content for each chapter or section:

Prompt: "Write the introduction for my eBook about (CHOSEN TOPIC AND TITLE   )."

Repeat this process for each chapter or section in your outline.

Design a cover and sales page:

Prompt: "Provide suggestions for designing an eye-catching cover for my eBook about (CHOSEN TOPIC AND TITLE   )."

Prompt: "Write a persuasive sales page copy for my eBook about (CHOSEN TOPIC AND TITLE   )."

Prompt: "Craft a ChatGPT prompt to help you with a specific aspect of your eBook creation process: 'Assist me in (eBook creation step) for my eBook about (CHOSEN TOPIC AND TITLE_____)."

NOTES

4. My Kid's Principal:

Prompt: "Write an email to your child's principal expressing your appreciation for the school's efforts in organizing a successful school event."

Response: "Subject: A Big Thank You for the Wonderful [Event Name]

Dear [Principal's Name],

I hope this email finds you well. I am [Your Name], the parent of [Your Child's Name] in [Child's Grade/Class]. I wanted to take a moment to express my heartfelt appreciation for the fantastic [Event Name] that the school organized recently.

The dedication and hard work of the staff, teachers, and volunteers were evident in every aspect of the event, from the planning and preparation to the seamless execution. It was clear that the event was enjoyable for the students and fostered a sense of community and camaraderie among parents and families.

I am grateful for your leadership and commitment to providing such enriching experiences for our children. [Your Child's Name] had a wonderful time and enthusiastically continues to talk about the event. As a parent, knowing that my child is in a nurturing environment that values their growth and development is reassuring.

Once again, thank you for your efforts and dedication to making [Event Name] a resounding success.

I am excited to see what other engaging activities the school has in store for the students in the future.

Warm regards, [Your Name]

[Your Contact Information]

Prompt: "As a reader, write an email to a school staff member or teacher, expressing your appreciation for their efforts in a specific situation. Use the following template as a guide:

'Dear (RECIPIENT'S NAME _____), I am (YOUR NAME _____) and (RELATIONSHIP TO THE SCHOOL _____). I wanted to express my (EMOTION _____) for (DESCRIBE THE SITUATION OR EVENT _____)."

NOTES

Example Prompt: "I'm an entrepreneur trying to improve my productivity. Can you provide some tips on how to stay focused and manage my time efficiently?"

Example Response: Certainly! Here are some tips for boosting productivity as an entrepreneur:

1. Set clear goals and prioritize tasks.
2. Break down projects into smaller manageable tasks.
3. Establish a routine and stick to it.
4. Allocate specific time blocks for different tasks.
5. Minimize distractions and create a focused work environment.
6. Utilize productivity tools and apps to stay organized.
7. Regularly review your progress and adjust as needed.
8. Don't forget to take breaks and maintain a healthy work-life balance.

Prompt: "As a reader, imagine you are seeking advice on a specific topic. Write a request for guidance using the following template: 'I'm a (YOUR OCCUPATION OR ROLE_____) trying to (YOUR GOAL OR CHALLENGE_____). Can you provide some tips on (WHAT YOU NEED HELP WITH_____)?'"

NOTES

Example Prompt: "Please provide a brief overview of affiliate marketing and how I can use AI-generated content to boost my affiliate marketing efforts."

Example Response: Affiliate marketing is a performance-based marketing strategy where you promote other companies' products or services and earn a commission for each sale made through your unique referral link. AI-generated content can help you create engaging and persuasive marketing materials, such as blog posts, social media updates, and email campaigns, to drive traffic and conversions for your

affiliate offers.

NOTES

Prompt: "As a reader, imagine you want to learn more about a specific subject. Write a request for information using the following template: 'Please provide a brief overview of (SUBJECT_____) and how I can (DESIRED OUTCOME_____)."'

NOTES

NOTES

Example Prompt: "What are some ways to use ChatGPT to enhance my freelance career?"

Example Response: ChatGPT can be a game-changer for freelancers in several ways, including:

1. Creating high-quality content for your clients.
2. Generating ideas for blog posts, articles, or social media updates.
3. Drafting and editing emails, proposals, and other business documents.
4. Assisting with research and summarizing information.
5. Brainstorming creative solutions for client projects.

Prompt: "As a reader, imagine you want to learn how a specific tool or resource can benefit your career. Write a request for information using the following template: 'What are some ways to use (TOOL OR RESOURCE_____) to enhance my (YOUR OCCUPATION OR ROLE_____) career?'"

NOTES

Example Prompt: "I'm looking for some 'Act as' prompts that I can use with ChatGPT. Can you provide a few examples?"

Example Response: Certainly! Here are some 'Act as' prompts to get you started:

1. Act as a personal finance advisor and provide budgeting tips.

2. Act as a nutritionist and suggest a healthy meal plan for a week.

3. Act as a career advisor and offer guidance on resume building.

4. Act as a travel agent and recommend a 7-day itinerary for a trip to Paris.

Prompt: "Create your own 'Act as' prompt by filling in the blanks: 'Act as an (EXPERT OR ROLE _____) and help me (TASK OR ADVICE YOU NEED _____).'"

NOTES

Prompt: "As a reader, imagine you want ChatGPT to act as a specific expert or role. Write a request for information using the following template: 'Act as an (EXPERT OR ROLE _____) and (TASK OR ADVICE YOU NEED _____).'"

NOTES

Example Prompt: "What are some limitations of ChatGPT that users should be aware of?"

Example Response: While ChatGPT is a powerful AI tool, it has some limitations, including:

1. It may generate plausible but incorrect or nonsensical answers
2. It is sensitive to input phrasing and may provide different responses for slightly rephrased questions.
3. It can be verbose and overuse certain phrases.
4. It may not always ask clarifying questions for ambiguous queries.
5. It can sometimes respond to harmful or biased prompts.

Prompt: "Identify a potential limitation or concern you may have about a specific tool or resource, using the following template: 'I am concerned about (TOOL OR RESOURCE_____) because it might (POTENTIAL LIMITATION OR CONCERN_____).'"

NOTES

NOTES

Prompt: "As a reader, imagine you want to learn about the limitations of a specific tool or resource. Write a request for information using the following template: 'What are some limitations of (TOOL OR RESOURCE_____) that users should be aware of?'"

NOTES

Example Prompt: "What are the key takeaways from using ChatGPT for my business or personal life?"

Example Response: Key takeaways from using ChatGPT include:

1. Improved productivity through faster content creation and idea generation.

2. Enhanced creativity with the help of AI-generated suggestions.

3. Streamlined communication by drafting and editing emails, proposals, and documents.

4. Access to expert knowledge and advice through 'Act as' prompts.

5. Personal and professional growth by leveraging AI to stay informed and up-to-date on various topics.

NOTES

Prompt: "As a reader, imagine you want to learn about the key takeaways or benefits of a specific tool or resource. Write a request for information using the following template: 'What are the key takeaways from using (TOOL OR RESOURCE_____) for my (BUSINESS OR PERSONAL _____) life?'"

NOTES

NOTES

Prompt: "Reflect on the benefits or key takeaways you have experienced from using a specific tool or resource. Write a statement using the following template: 'Using (TOOL OR RESOURCE_____) has helped me (BENEFIT OR KEY TAKEAWAY_____) in my (BUSINESS OR PERSONAL_____) life.'"

NOTES

5. Coder for Web Development:

Prompt: "Write an introduction for a beginner-friendly tutorial on learning HTML and CSS for web development."

Response: "Hey there, aspiring web developers! Welcome to our Beginner's Guide to HTML and CSS. My name is [Your Name], and I'll be your instructor on this exciting journey into the world of web development. In this tutorial, we'll cover everything you need to know to build your very first website from scratch. We'll start with the basics of HTML, the language used to structure web pages, and then move on to CSS, which allows you to style and design your site. By the end of this tutorial, you'll have a solid foundation in web development and be well on your way to creating stunning websites.

So, let's get started, and remember- practice makes perfect!
#webdevelopment #learnhtmlcss "

Prompt: "As a reader, think about your own experience with HTML and CSS. Write a brief reflection on what you found challenging or interesting and how you plan to apply this knowledge in the future. Use the following template to guide your response: 'When I first started learning HTML and CSS, I found (challenge or interesting aspect) to be (difficult/easy/fascinating/etc.). Moving forward, I plan to use this knowledge to (personal goal or application).'"

NOTES

As you continue to explore and experiment with ChatGPT, remember to maintain a conversational tone and provide clear instructions to engage your audience.

Encourage them to ask questions, offer feedback, and share their experiences to foster a sense of community and create a more enriching learning experience for everyone involved.

Don't forget to grab your free prompt guide; it will help you along this journey that you are embarking on. Don't do ChatGPT alone!

Chapter 5

The Superhuman Freelancer's Secret Weapon: How ChatGPT Can Level Up Your Game

---

Outline
- Using ChatGPT for research, content creation, and more
- Boosting efficiency with AI tools
- Marketing your skills as an AI-powered freelancer

As a freelancer, you're always looking for ways to work smarter, not harder. In this chapter, we'll explore how ChatGPT can help you do just that. Transforming your work process and making you an even more efficient, effective, and valuable professional. Now let's dive in and see how ChatGPT can become your secret weapon.

Using ChatGPT for research, content creation, and more:
Imagine being able to create a blog post or a piece of content in minutes rather than hours. By using ChatGPT, you can achieve this level of efficiency. By feeding the AI specific details and instructions, you'll have a powerful content generation tool at your fingertips. But remember, ChatGPT is here to support and enhance your skills, not replace them. You still need to review and refine the generated content to make sure it meets your client's expectations.

Boosting efficiency with AI tools:
Take a moment to think about how much time you spend on content creation, research, and brainstorming. Imagine cutting that time in half or even more; with ChatGPT, you can do just that. By using AI to assist with these tasks, you free up more time to focus on other aspects of your business, like marketing, networking, and improving your skills.

Marketing your skills as an AI-powered freelancer:

As a freelancer, you know that marketing your skills is key to building your reputation and attracting clients. By incorporating ChatGPT into your services, you can showcase your ability to deliver high-quality work quickly and efficiently. Share examples of content created without ChatGPT and content created with it to show potential clients the difference in quality and speed.

Let's explore some practical examples of how you can use ChatGPT in your freelance work:

1. **Ghostwriting:** With ChatGPT, you can generate content quickly and efficiently, allowing you to take on more ghostwriting projects. Just give the AI the necessary details, and it will produce a draft for you to review and refine. This way, you can focus on adding your unique touch and expertise to the content.

2. **Marketing strategies:** If you're a marketing freelancer, ChatGPT can help you create marketing strategies for your clients. Feed the AI information about your client's business, goals, and target audience, and it will generate ideas for you to review and adjust as needed.

3. **Web development:** As a web developer, you can use ChatGPT to generate code snippets, create website copy, or even assist in brainstorming ideas for new features or designs.

Now, let's put ChatGPT to the test. We've provided some prompts for you to practice with. Fill in the blanks to customize the prompts, then use ChatGPT to generate responses.

Ghostwriting Example:

Your Prompt: "Write an introduction to an article about (YOUR TOPIC_____) using ChatGPT."

Response: (ChatGPT's introduction).

NOTES

NOTES

Marketing Strategy Example:

Prompt: "Help me create a marketing strategy for (CLIENT'S BUSINESS_____) using ChatGPT."

Response: (ChatGPT's marketing strategy).

NOTES

Your Prompt: "Help me create a marketing strategy for (YOUR CLIENT'S BUSINESS_____) using ChatGPT."

NOTES

NOTES

Web Development Example:

Prompt: "Generate a code snippet for a responsive navigation menu using ChatGPT."

Response: (ChatGPT's code snippet).

NOTES

Your Prompt: "Generate a code snippet for (your desired feature) using ChatGPT."

Conclusion:

By incorporating ChatGPT into your freelance work, you'll be able to enhance your skills, increase your efficiency, and provide even more value to your clients. Remember, ChatGPT is here to support you, not replace you. It's essential to review and refine the AI-generated content to ensure it meets your client's expectations. By doing so, you'll be on your way to becoming a superhuman freelancer, ready to tackle even more projects and grow your business.

Let's start experimenting with ChatGPT today and see how this powerful AI tool can help you level up your game. Embrace the technology, and let it amplify your already amazing skills. Your clients will be amazed by your newfound efficiency, and your business will thrive. Now, go forth and conquer the freelance world with ChatGPT by your side!

NOTES

Chapter 6

Let's Get Creative: Fun with "Act as" Prompts

Outline
- How to use "act as" prompts for engaging content
- Examples of enjoyable and useful "act as" prompts
- Tips for creating your own unique "act as" prompts

Introduction:

"Act as" prompts are a fantastic way to get more creative, engaging, and personalized content from ChatGPT. By using these prompts, you can bring a specific persona, tone, or expertise to your content by making it more interesting and dynamic. This chapter will explore various "act as" prompts and how to use them effectively. Plus, we'll provide a template for you to create your own unique "act as" prompts!

- Home Improvement Expert (Contractor)
- Coffee Expert
- Life Coach
- Business Founder of a Start-up
- Angel Investor
- Spanish Tour Guide
- Negotiation Coach
- Business Brand Consultant
- Personal Brand Consultant
- Motivational Speaker Coach
- Personal Financial Advisor
- IT Expert
- Self-help Coach
- Professional Resume Writer
- Book Advisor/Geek
- Stock Broker
- Mental Health Professional

- Personal Fitness Instructor

Life Coach

Prompt: "Act as a life coach and advise me on setting achievable goals."

Response: "As a life coach, I recommend breaking your goals down into smaller, manageable steps. Start by defining your long-term goal and then create a series of short-term objectives that will lead you there. Make sure to set SMART goals (Specific, Measurable, Achievable, Relevant, and Time-bound) to increase your chances of success. Remember to celebrate your small victories along the way and adjust your plan as needed."

Startup Founder

Prompt: "Act as a successful startup founder and provide tips on building a strong team."

Response: "As a startup founder, I can tell you that building a strong team is crucial for success. Look for individuals who share your vision and are passionate about your mission. Prioritize soft skills like communication, collaboration, and adaptability, as these are often more important than technical skills alone. Finally, create an inclusive and supportive company culture to foster growth, development, and long-lasting commitment from your team members."

Home Improvement Expert

Prompt: "Act as a home improvement expert and suggest ways to increase a home's value on a budget."

Response: "As a home improvement expert, I recommend focusing on high-impact, low-cost projects. Start by improving curb appeal with fresh landscaping, a clean exterior, and a freshly painted front door. Inside, focus on updating kitchens and bathrooms with new fixtures, hardware, and a fresh coat of paint. Lastly, declutter and depersonalize your space to create a clean, inviting atmosphere for potential buyers."

Coffee Expert

Prompt: "Act as a coffee expert and recommend the best brewing method for a rich and flavorful cup."

Response: "As a coffee expert, I highly recommend the pour-over brewing method for a rich and flavorful cup. This method allows you to control the water temperature, brew time, and coffee-to-water ratio, resulting in a clean, balanced, and nuanced taste. Use freshly roasted and ground beans, a gooseneck kettle for precise pouring, and a quality pour-over dripper like a Hario V60 or Chemex for the best results."

Create Your Own "Act as" Prompts Template:

Now that you've seen some examples of "act as" prompts, it's time to create your own! Use this template as a guide:

Nutritionist

Prompt: "Act as a nutritionist and provide tips on maintaining a balanced diet."

Response: "As a nutritionist, I recommend following these tips to maintain a balanced diet: include a variety of fruits, vegetables, whole grains, lean proteins, and healthy fats in your meals; practice portion control; stay hydrated; limit processed foods, added sugars, and saturated fats; and pay attention to your body's hunger and fullness cues. Remember, moderation and diversity are key to a healthy, balanced diet."

Travel Agent

Prompt: "Act as a travel agent and give advice on planning an unforgettable vacation."

Response: "As a travel agent, I suggest starting by setting a budget and choosing a destination that aligns with your interests and travel goals. Research the best time to visit, considering factors like weather, peak tourist seasons, and local events. Plan your itinerary, including must-see attractions, local experiences, and downtime for relaxation. Book accommodations, flights, and any necessary transportation in advance. And most importantly, be flexible and open to new experiences during your trip."

Pet Expert (Dog Whisperer)

Prompt: "Act as a dog whisperer and share tips on how to train a well-behaved dog."

Response: "As a dog whisperer, I believe that positive reinforcement, patience, and consistency are the keys to successful dog training. Start by teaching basic commands like sit, stay, and come using rewards like treats or praise. Establish mealtimes, walks, and playtime routines to provide structure and predictability. Be patient and consistent in your approach, and avoid punishment-based methods. Remember, building a strong bond and mutual trust with your dog is the foundation for effective training."

DJ

Prompt: "Act as a DJ and explain how to create a perfect playlist for a party."

Response: "As a DJ, the key to creating a perfect party playlist is to understand your audience and the event's vibe. Start by selecting a mix of genres and tempos that cater to diverse tastes while maintaining a consistent energy level. Be sure to include popular hits and crowd-pleasers, but don't be afraid to throw in lesser-known tracks and remixes to keep things fresh. Pay attention to the flow and transitions between songs, and be prepared to adjust your playlist on the fly based on the crowd's response."

Now that we've provided additional examples use the previous response's template to craft your own "Act as" prompts. Remember to think about your content's persona, tone, mission, and expectations, and let your creativity flow as you explore the endless possibilities with ChatGPT.

1. Choose a persona or expertise: _____

2. Define the tone or style:

   _____

3. Set a mission or goal for the content:

   _____

4. Establish specific expectations: _____

Now it's your turn! Here are four fill-in-the-blank spaces for you to create your own "act as" prompts. Use the examples above as inspiration and consider the role, tone, influence, mission, and expectations you want to convey.

Act as a _____ and provide advice on

_____

Response: _____

Act as a _____ and describe your

_____

Response: _____

Act as a _____ and share tips on

_____

Response:_____

Act as an _____ and explain the importance of _____ and how to _____

Response: _____

With these fill-in-the-blank prompts, you can practice and refine your skills in creating engaging and effective "act as" prompts. Keep this book handy as a reference guide, and remember to think creatively and have fun with the process!

Once you have these elements in place, craft your "Act as" prompt and let ChatGPT bring your unique vision to life! Enjoy the process of experimenting with different personas and expertise, and watch as your content becomes more engaging and personalized. Happy prompting!

Expanding on the "act as" prompts list, let's explore a few more examples to spark your creativity and help you get even more out of ChatGPT.

Don't forget to grab your free prompt guide. It will help you along this journey that you are embarking on. Don't do ChatGPT alone! Click the link to get yours
https://chatgptpromptbook.com/freebie.

Chapter 7

What ChatGPT Can't Do: Understanding Its Limitations

Outline
- Recognizing the limitations of ChatGPT
- Overcoming these limitations with human-AI collaboration
- Preparing for future improvements in AI technology

By now, you're likely feeling excited about the countless possibilities that ChatGPT offers. It's an incredible tool that can save time, boost productivity, and spark creativity.

However, it's essential to recognize that ChatGPT, like any AI technology, has its limitations. In this chapter, we'll discuss some of these limitations, how human-AI collaboration can help overcome them, and what to expect as AI technology continues to advance.

1. Recognizing the limitations of ChatGPT

While ChatGPT is incredibly powerful, it's not perfect. Here are a few limitations you should be aware of:

- It might generate content that is irrelevant, nonsensical, or even offensive.
- It might not always understand the context or specific nuances of your prompt.
- It can sometimes be overly verbose or repetitive.
- It doesn't have the ability to fact-check or verify the accuracy of the information it provides.

2. Overcoming these limitations with human-AI collaboration

Despite these limitations, ChatGPT can still be a valuable asset when used effectively.

Here's how you can overcome some of these limitations through human-AI collaboration:

- Always review the content generated by ChatGPT and make necessary edits to ensure accuracy, relevance, and readability.
- Refine your prompts by providing more context, being more specific, or rephrasing your question to get a better response.
- Use ChatGPT as a starting point, and then rely on your expertise and research to enhance and polish the content.

3. Preparing for future improvements in AI technology

AI technology is continuously evolving, and we can expect many of these limitations to be addressed in future iterations of ChatGPT and other AI tools. As these tools become more sophisticated, the collaboration between humans and AI will only grow stronger.

It's important to stay informed about advancements in AI technology and be open to adapting your approach as the technology continues to improve.

4. Balancing expectations: Knowing when to rely on ChatGPT and when to seek human expertise.

Understanding the limitations of ChatGPT also means knowing when to rely on it and when to seek human expertise. Here are some guidelines to help you find the right balance:

- Use ChatGPT for brainstorming, ideation, and content generation, but always involve human expertise to ensure quality and accuracy.
- Rely on ChatGPT for automating repetitive tasks, but remember that complex or nuanced projects may require human judgment and decision-making.
- When using ChatGPT for research, always cross-check information with reliable sources to ensure accuracy.

5. Staying ethical and responsible with AI technology

As you leverage the power of ChatGPT, staying ethical and responsible is essential. Here are some tips for using ChatGPT in a manner that respects privacy, intellectual property, and social norms:

- Do not use ChatGPT to create content that promotes hate speech, violence, or discrimination.
- Ensure that any generated content does not infringe on copyright or intellectual property rights.
- When using ChatGPT for professional purposes, always disclose that AI-generated content has been used and edited by humans to maintain transparency and trust with clients or audiences.

6. Embracing the future: Staying up-to-date with AI advancements

As AI technology continues to advance, it's crucial to stay informed about new developments, improvements, and best practices. By keeping up-to-date with the latest advancements in AI, you can ensure that you're making the most of ChatGPT and other AI tools. Consider subscribing to AI-focused newsletters, attending webinars, and participating in online forums or communities to stay at the forefront of AI technology.

In summary, while ChatGPT is an incredibly powerful tool, it's essential to recognize and understand its limitations. By collaborating with AI, refining your prompts, and staying up-to-date with advancements in AI technology, you can overcome these limitations and maximize the benefits of ChatGPT. Embrace the exciting world of AI and enjoy the journey as you continue to explore and learn about the potential of ChatGPT and other AI tools.

Don't forget to grab your free prompt guide. It will help you along this journey that you are embarking on. Don't do ChatGPT alone! Click the link to get yours https://chatgptpromptbook.com/freebie.

Chapter 8

Looking Ahead: The Exciting Future of AI and ChatGPT

Outline
- The potential of AI and ChatGPT in the years to come.
- The Role of AI in Shaping the Future of Freelancing and Startups.
- Encouraging readers to stay informed and adapt to AI advancements.

The potential of AI and ChatGPT in the years to come

As you've seen throughout this book, AI and ChatGPT have the power to revolutionize how we work, create, and interact. You can expect even more advanced AI models in the years to come. With its enhanced capabilities to understand context, generate more nuanced content, and collaborate seamlessly with humans, these advancements will undoubtedly unlock new opportunities and transform countless industries, which include freelancing, startups, and beyond.

The role of AI in shaping the future of freelancing and startups

As AI progresses, freelancers and startups can expect a world of new possibilities. AI-driven tools like ChatGPT can help level the playing field for small businesses. Empowering them to compete with larger organizations by streamlining tasks, improving productivity, and fostering creativity. The ability to harness AI's power will increasingly become a defining factor in the success of freelancers and startups, enabling them to deliver exceptional work more efficiently and cost-effectively.

Staying informed and adapting to AI advancements

To make the most of AI's potential and stay ahead of the curve, it's vital for you to remain informed about the latest advancements and adapt to the ever-changing landscape. By embracing a mindset of continuous learning and staying open to new possibilities, you can unlock the full potential of AI and ChatGPT in your work and personal life. Consider joining online forums, participating in workshops, and networking with fellow professionals to share experiences, insights, and best practices.

Thank you and a reminder to claim your freebie

We want to take a moment to thank you for joining us on this incredible journey through the world of AI and ChatGPT. We hope this book has provided valuable insights, practical tips, and inspiration to harness the power of AI in your professional and personal life.

As a token of our appreciation, don't forget to claim your freebie by following the instructions provided earlier in the book. This exclusive bonus will help you dive even deeper into the world of ChatGPT and make the most of its capabilities.

Here's to a bright future with AI and ChatGPT at your side, empowering you to reach new heights and transform how you work, create, and innovate.

Grab your Freebie at https://chatgptpromptbook.com/freebie '

Scan the Qr Code to get your Freebie

NOTES

Appendix

ChatGPT Lingo Decoded and Resources Just for You

Section 1: ChatGPT Lingo Decoded

As you dive deeper into the world of ChatGPT, you may encounter new terms and concepts that are unfamiliar to you. To help you navigate this exciting new world, we've compiled a list of essential ChatGPT lingo decoded for you. This section includes definitions of key terms such as prompt, token, and beam search, as well as a breakdown of how ChatGPT works.

Section 2: Glossary of Essential AI and ChatGPT Terms

In addition to ChatGPT-specific terms, you'll also encounter a variety of essential AI and machine learning terms. In this section, we've created a glossary that covers essential terms such as artificial intelligence, deep learning, and natural language processing.

Understanding these terms is crucial to developing a strong foundation in AI and ChatGPT, so be sure to take the time to review this section carefully.

Section 3: Curated List of Resources: Books, Courses, and Websites for Further Learning

To help you continue your ChatGPT journey, we've compiled a curated list of resources, including books, courses, and websites for further learning. This section includes recommendations for books on AI and machine learning, online courses on ChatGPT and related topics, and websites and blogs that offer in-depth insights into the latest developments in the field. Whether you're a beginner or an experienced AI practitioner, these resources are sure to enhance your understanding and deepen your knowledge of ChatGPT and the world of AI.

Request for the appendix of the book:

We highly recommend referring to the appendix of this book as you embark on your ChatGPT journey. This section includes ChatGPT lingo decoded, a glossary of essential AI and ChatGPT terms, and a curated list of resources to help you continue your learning. By utilizing these tools, you'll be well-equipped to master ChatGPT and harnessits full potential.

Section 1: ChatGPT Lingo Decoded and Resources Just for You As you begin your ChatGPT journey, it's essential to understand the language and terms used in the field of artificial intelligence. This section will help you decode the ChatGPT lingo and provide you with resources to navigate your way through the world of AI.

1.1 ChatGPT Terminology

* **Language Model:** A computer program that can generate human-like text basedon a given prompt.
* **Fine-tuning:** The process of training a pre-existing language model on a specificdataset to improve its performance on a particular task.
* **Prompt:** The starting point or seed that is given to a language model to generatetext.
* **API:** An application programming interface, a set of protocols, routines, and toolsfor building software applications.
* **OpenAI:** An AI research laboratory consisting of the for-profit corporation OpenAILP and its parent company, the non-profit OpenAI Inc.

2. ChatGPT Resources

As you begin your journey with ChatGPT, it's crucial to have access to the right resources. Here are some recommended resources to help you get started:

* **OpenAI API documentation:** The official documentation for the OpenAI API thatprovides detailed instructions on how to use ChatGPT.
* **OpenAI Community Forum:** A community-driven forum where you can ask questions, share ideas, and connect with other users of ChatGPT.
* **GPT-3 Playground:** An online platform that allows you to experiment with ChatGPT's capabilities and see the results in real-time.
* **Hugging Face:** A library of pre-trained language models, including ChatGPT, thatcan be fine-tuned and used for various NLP tasks.
* **ChatGPT Github:** A repository of code and resources related to ChatGPT,including tutorials, examples, and research papers.

3. ChatGPT Troubleshooting

As with any technology, there may be hiccups along the way. Here are some commonissues and troubleshooting tips to help you resolve them:

1. **Error messages:** If you encounter an error message, try rephrasing your promptor changing the parameters to see if that solves the issue.
2. **Slow response time:** If ChatGPT is taking too long to respond, try reducing thenumber of tokens or increasing the batch size.
3. **API connection issues:** If you're having trouble connecting to the API, double-check your authentication credentials and ensure that you have a stable internet connection.

ChatGPT Lingo Decoded and Resources Just for You As you start your ChatGPT journey, you may come across some terms that are unfamiliar to you. To help you decode the lingo and navigate the world of ChatGPT withease, we've compiled a list of essential terms and resources just for you.

- **Language Model** - A language model is an AI system that can generatehuman-like text based on a given prompt.
- **OpenAI** - OpenAI is an AI research laboratory consisting of the for-profit OpenAI LP and the non-profit OpenAI Inc. The laboratory is dedicated to advancing AI in away that is safe and beneficial to humanity.
- **API** - An API (application programming interface) is a set of protocols and toolsused to build software applications.
- **Prompt** - A prompt is a set of instructions or guidelines used to generate text using a language model.
- **Finetuning** - Finetuning is the process of adapting a pre-trained language modelto a specific task or domain by further training it on a new dataset.
- **Corpus** - A corpus is a collection of text used to train language models.
- **Neural Network** - A neural network is a type of AI system inspired by the structureand function of the human brain, which is composed of interconnected neurons.
- **Transformer Architecture** - The Transformer architecture is a type of neural network used in language modeling that has been shown to achieve state-of-

the-art results in many natural language processing tasks.

- **OpenAI's ChatGPT Documentation** - This is the official documentation forChatGPT and provides detailed instructions on how to use the tool.
- **OpenAI's Github Repository** - The Github repository contains the source code forChatGPT, as well as pre-trained models and other resources.
- **ChatGPT Community Forum** - This forum is a place where ChatGPT users candiscuss the tool, share tips and tricks, and ask for help.
- **ChatGPT Tutorials** - There are several tutorials available online that providestep-by-step instructions on how to use ChatGPT for various tasks.
- **ChatGPT Courses** - There are also several online courses available that teach you how to use ChatGPT for specific applications.

We hope this glossary and list of resources will help you on your ChatGPT journey. If you have any questions or need further assistance, feel free to consult the resources provided or ask for help in the ChatGPT community forum.

Section 2: Glossary of Essential AI and ChatGPT Terms

As you begin your journey with ChatGPT, it's essential to understand the key terminology related to AI and language models. This glossary will help you navigate the jargon and understand the essential terms.

- **Artificial Intelligence (AI):** The simulation of human intelligence processes bymachines, especially computer systems.
- **Machine Learning:** The study of computer algorithms that improve automaticallythrough experience.
- **Natural Language Processing (NLP):** The ability of computers to understand, interpret, and generate human language.
- **Deep Learning:** A subset of machine learning where artificial neural networks, algorithms inspired by the human brain, learn from large amounts of data.
- **Language Model:** A type of artificial intelligence that uses probability and statistical techniques to predict the likelihood of the next word or sentence in a given context.
- **Chatbot:** A computer program designed to simulate conversation with human

users, especially over the Internet.

- **API (Application Programming Interface):** A set of protocols, routines, and toolsfor building software and applications.
- **Prompt:** The initial text or question given to ChatGPT to generate a response.
- **GPT (Generative Pre-trained Transformer):** A type of language model developedby OpenAI that uses deep learning to generate human-like text.
- **Fine-tuning:** The process of training a pre-trained language model like GPT toadapt to a specific task or domain.
- **Artificial Intelligence (AI):** The development of computer systems that can perform tasks that would typically require human intelligence, such as perception, speech recognition, decision-making, and language translation.
- **Machine Learning (ML):** A subset of AI that involves teaching machines to learnfrom data, rather than explicitly programming them to perform a specific task.
- **Natural Language Processing (NLP):** A subset of AI that focuses on the interaction between humans and machines using natural language. NLP is the foundation of ChatGPT's ability to generate human-like text.
- **Deep Learning:** A subset of ML that involves using neural networks with manylayers to perform complex tasks, such as image and speech recognition.
- **Neural Network:** A set of algorithms modeled after the structure of the human brain that can learn from data and make predictions.
- **Prompt:** The input given to ChatGPT that serves as a starting point for generatinghuman-like text.
- **Fine-Tuning:** The process of training ChatGPT on specific data to improve its ability to generate text related to a particular topic or task.
- **Transformer Architecture:** The neural network architecture used by ChatGPT, which allows it to generate high-quality text by modeling the relationships between words and phrases in a text corpus.

1. **Bias:** In AI, bias refers to the tendency of an AI system to produce results that aresystematically prejudiced against certain groups or individuals.
2. **Explainability:** The ability of an AI system to explain how it arrived at a particulardecision or prediction.

3. **Artificial Intelligence (AI)** - The ability of machines to perform tasks that typically require human intelligence, such as recognizing speech, making decisions, andlearning.

4. **Machine Learning (ML)** - A subset of AI that involves training machines to learnfrom data without being explicitly programmed.

5. **Natural Language Processing (NLP)** - A subfield of AI that deals with the interaction between computers and human language, including tasks such as speech recognition and language translation.

6. **Neural Network** - A computer system modeled after the structure of the humanbrain, designed to recognize patterns and learn from data.

7. **Deep Learning** - A type of ML that involves training neural networks with multiple layers, allowing for more complex tasks such as image and speech recognition.

8. **GPT (Generative Pre-trained Transformer)** - An advanced language model developed by OpenAI, capable of generating human-like text based on a given prompt.

9. **API (Application Programming Interface)** - A set of protocols and tools used to build software applications and enable communication between different systems.

10. **Prompt** - The text used to initiate the generation of text by a language model such as GPT.

11. **Fine-tuning** - The process of adapting a pre-trained language model such as GPTto a specific task or domain, by providing it with additional training data.

12. **Token** - A unit of language used by a language model such as GPT, typically a word or punctuation mark.

By familiarizing yourself with these essential terms, you'll be better equipped to navigatethe world of AI and ChatGPT, communicate effectively with developers and other professionals, and make the most of this incredible technology.

Section 3: Curated List of Resources for Further Learning

As you continue to explore the world of AI and ChatGPT, it's important to have access to reliable and relevant resources. In this section, we've curated a list of books, courses, and websites that can help you deepen your understanding and hone your skills.

Books:
1. "Hands-On Machine Learning with Scikit-Learn, Keras, and TensorFlow" by Aurelien Geron
2. "Deep Learning" by Yoshua Bengio, Ian Goodfellow, and Aaron Courville
3. "The Hundred-Page Machine Learning Book" by Andriy Burkov
4. "Artificial Intelligence: A Modern Approach" by Stuart Russell and Peter Norvig
5. "The AI Delusion" by Gary Smith
6. "The Singularity is Near: When Humans Transcend Biology" by Ray Kurzweil
7. "Superintelligence: Paths, Dangers, Strategies" by Nick Bostrom
8. "Machine Learning Yearning" by Andrew Ng
9. "Artificial Intelligence: A Modern Approach" by Stuart Russell and Peter Norvig

Courses:
1. Coursera's Machine Learning Course by Andrew Ng
2. Stanford University's CS221: Artificial Intelligence: Principles and Techniques
3. Udacity's AI Programming with Python Nanodegree Program
4. Fast.ai's Practical Deep Learning for Coders
5. MIT's Introduction to Deep Learning
6. "Machine Learning" by Andrew Ng on Coursera
7. "Introduction to Artificial Intelligence with Python" by IBM on Coursera
8. "AI For Everyone" by Andrew Ng on Coursera

Websites:
1. **OpenAI** - The creators of ChatGPT offer various resources, including a blog, research papers, and technical documentation.
2. **Kaggle** - A community for data scientists and machine learning enthusiasts to explore and share their work.
3. **TensorFlow** - An open-source platform for machine learning and deep

learning.

4. **GitHub** - A platform for sharing code, including AI-related projects and repositories.

5. **AI-ML Wiki** - A wiki-style website with resources and information on AI and machine learning.

6. **MachineLearningMastery.com:** A comprehensive resource for machine learning, deeplearning, and artificial intelligence.

7. **KDnuggets.com:** A popular data science community and resource hub, featuring articles,tutorials, and industry news.

These resources are just the tip of the iceberg, but they can provide an excellent starting point foranyone looking to expand their knowledge and skills in the field of AI and ChatGPT. Happy learning!

To read the freebie click; https://chatgptpromptbook.com/freebie '

Scan the Qr Code to get your Freebie

NOTES

NOTES

NOTES